LINCOLNWOOD PUBLIC LIBRARY
3 1242 00168 0868

W9-AQV-198

# The Boston Massacre

CORNERSTONES OF FREEDOM™

SECOND SERIES

Andrew Santella

**Children's Press®**
A Division of Scholastic Inc.
New York • Toronto • London • Auckland • Sydney
Mexico City • New Delhi • Hong Kong
Danbury, Connecticut

Photographs ©2004: Art Resource, NY: 6 (Biblioteque Nationale, Paris, France), 3 (Wallach Division, New York Public Library, New York, NY, U.S.A.); Bridgeman Art Library International Ltd., London/New York: 18 (Massachusetts Historical Society, Boston, MA, USA), 33 (Museum of Fine Arts, Boston, Massachusetts, USA); Brown Brothers: 4, 11 bottom, 32, 36, 45 center; Commonwealth of Massachusetts Art Commission/Sir Francis Bernard by Giovanni Battista Troccoli after John Singleton Copley, Massachusetts State House Art Collection: 15; Corbis Images: 28, 30 (Bettmann), 27 (Fleming); Hulton|Archive/Getty Images: 16, 19, 34, 45 bottom; Mary Evans Picture Library: 13, 20; North Wind Picture Archives: cover bottom, 5, 7, 8, 9, 10 top, 10 bottom, 12, 14, 23, 24, 29, 31, 35, 39, 40, 44 top right, 44 bottom, 44 top left, 45 top; Social Law Library, Boston: 41; Stock Montage, Inc.: cover top, 11 top, 17, 21, 25, 26.

Library of Congress Cataloging-in-Publication Data

Santella, Andrew.

The Boston Massacre / Andrew Santella.

p. cm. — (Cornerstones of freedom. Second series)

Summary: Discusses the events leading up to the Boston Massacre, including the Sugar and Stamp Acts, and the aftermath of the massacre.

Includes bibliographical references (p. ) and index.

ISBN 0-516-24226-1

1. Boston Massacre, 1770—Juvenile literature. [1. Boston Massacre, 1770.] I. Title. II. Series.

E215.4.S36 2004

973.3'113—dc21

2003009095



1 2 3 4 5 6 7 8 9 10 R 13 12 11 10 09 08 07 06 05 04

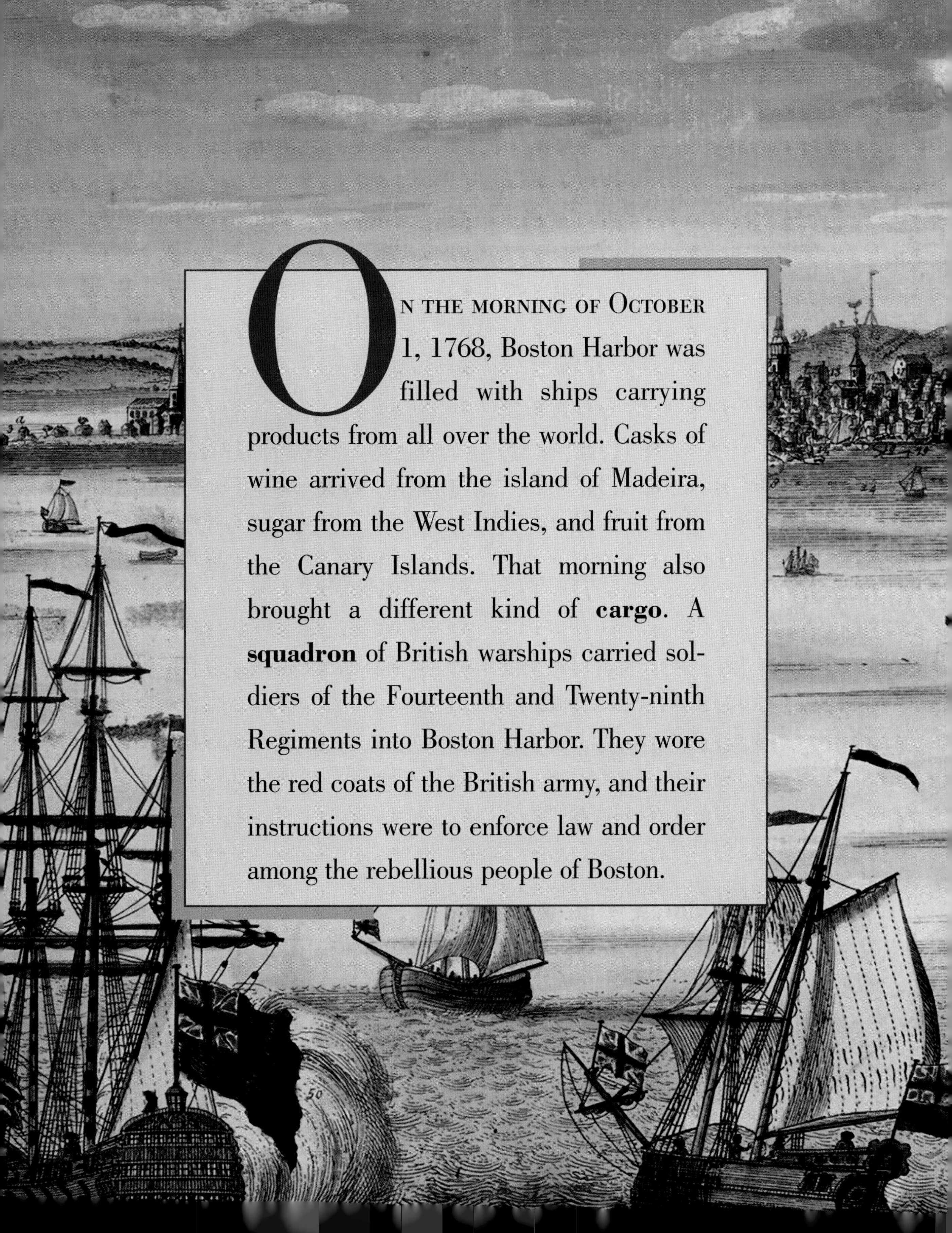

On the morning of October 1, 1768, Boston Harbor was filled with ships carrying products from all over the world. Casks of wine arrived from the island of Madeira, sugar from the West Indies, and fruit from the Canary Islands. That morning also brought a different kind of **cargo**. A **squadron** of British warships carried soldiers of the Fourteenth and Twenty-ninth Regiments into Boston Harbor. They wore the red coats of the British army, and their instructions were to enforce law and order among the rebellious people of Boston.

The troops began landing at Boston's Long Wharf that afternoon, ready to impress the people of Boston with a show of British army splendor. They formed columns and began marching up King Street. With flags flying and drums sounding, they headed into the heart of Boston.

Some Bostonians were relieved to see British soldiers marching into town. The city had been disturbed by violent **mobs** in recent months, and the troops promised a return to order. But others were not so welcoming. One leader of Boston's rebellious patriot **faction** was heard to boast that "we will destroy every soldier that dares put his foot on shore."

**British warships arrived in Boston Harbor on October 1, 1768.**

**With much fanfare, British troops entered Boston to enforce taxation and other colonial legislation.**

**This illustration shows a view of Boston in the 1700s.**

By late afternoon, the soldiers had completed their parade through the streets of Boston. In the months to come, those streets would witness still more trouble.

## BOSTON AND THE BRITISH

Boston was among the oldest cities in Great Britain's American colonies. (A colony is a territory controlled by a nation from a great distance.) Boston was founded in 1630, just ten years after the Pilgrims landed at nearby Plymouth.

By 1768, it was a bustling city of about 15,000 people and the center of political life in Massachusetts.

As in the other British colonies, the people of Massachusetts were proud to consider themselves loyal citizens of the British empire. They were used to having a say in their own government. They elected representatives who helped govern the colony. Those representatives worked with a colonial governor appointed by the king to run the colony.

The relationship between Britain and the American colonists, however, began to sour in the 1760s. The trouble began at the end of the French and Indian War, when the colonists helped Great Britain fight a long war with France for control of North America. The war ended in a complete British victory.

The long and expensive war, however, had drained the British **treasury**. In addition, the British government still had to bear the costs of governing and defending its vast new territories. To bring in the money it needed, the government would have to raise taxes—the payments people make to help support government services.

**THE FRENCH AND INDIAN WAR**

**As a result of the French and Indian War, Great Britain gained control of former French territory in Canada, the Great Lakes region, and the Mississippi River valley. This meant that Great Britain controlled all of North America east of the Mississippi River.**

**The French and Indian War was the result of colonial rivalry between France and Great Britain. Although Great Britain won the war, it was a costly victory.**

**When the British government imposed new taxes on the colonies, many colonists responded with riots and protests.**

The British government was already heavily taxing the people of England. So when still more funds were needed, there was only one place to look. The British government decided to begin taxing its American colonies.

The plan to impose new taxes on the colonists made perfect sense to the British. After all, the war with France had been fought partly to protect the colonies from the French and their Indian allies. British lawmakers reasoned that since the colonies were enjoying the benefits of victory, it was only fair for them to pay their share of taxes and other fees. Beginning in 1764, Parliament (the British lawmaking body) passed a series of tax and trade laws that affected the American colonies. The colonists had no say in any of these new laws, and greeted each with howls of protest. Bostonians played a leading role in the protests.

## SUGAR AND STAMPS

The first of the new laws was the Sugar Act of 1764. It set tougher standards for the enforcement of laws governing **imported** goods. Existing laws already called for colonists to pay duties, or taxes, on imported goods such as sugar, molasses, and coffee. However, many colonial merchants had figured out ways to avoid paying such duties. The British government cracked down on the enforcement of import duties with the passing of the Sugar Act. The British

**Counting-room workers kept track of money matters in the shipping business.**

Stamps such as this one were issued for a variety of legal and official documents.

Navy was ordered to more strictly enforce the payment of duties, leaving colonists with no choice but to pay up.

The Sugar Act cost New England merchants dearly, and many protested the new law. This was only the beginning, however. In 1765, Parliament passed the Stamp Act. This new law required a wide range of documents to carry a royal stamp, with funds from the sale of the stamps going to the British treasury. The stamps were required on newspapers, playing cards, college diplomas, legal contracts, liquor licenses, financial documents, and dozens of other kinds of printed material. For the first time, colonists had to pay for royal stamps to cover all these documents. Not surprisingly, the Stamp Act proved very unpopular with colonists.

## THE STAMP ACT CONGRESS

**To discuss resisting the Stamp Act, the Massachusetts legislature called for a congress of representatives from each of Britain's American colonies. The Stamp Act Congress met in New York City in October 1765, with delegates from nine colonies attending. The Congress declared that freeborn Englishmen could not be taxed without their consent. Because the colonists were not represented in Parliament, any tax imposed on them without the consent of colonial legislatures was unconstitutional.**

The colonists formed groups—both large and small—to discuss ways to resist British authority.

The Stamp Act was not the first tax American colonists had to pay. However, previous taxes had been imposed by local colonial governments, which were made up of the colonists themselves. The Stamp Act was the work of the British Parliament, in which the colonists had no representation. Colonists argued that it was unfair for Parliament to tax them.

Boston colonists became outraged after reading the terms of the Stamp Act.

To protest the Stamp Act, Boston merchants organized a **boycott**, refusing to sell goods imported from England. Opponents of the British taxes formed a group called the Sons of Liberty to take action against the laws. Protests against the law turned violent. On August 14, 1765, a mob attacked the home of Andrew Oliver, a local official who had been placed in charge of selling the stamps. Oliver's home was destroyed, and he resigned his job the next day. Days later, a mob attacked the home of another royal official.

A mob chased Andrew Oliver, a Loyalist who was appointed distributor of tax stamps.

## PATRIOTS AND LOYALISTS

Public opinion about British policies in the American colonies was divided. Patriots, or radicals, worked to defeat British policies. Some even took the first steps toward American independence from Great Britain. Loyalists, or tories, continued to support the British government's rule in the colonies.

Under the pressure of such protests in Boston and elsewhere, Parliament finally **repealed** the Stamp Act in 1766. Colonists celebrated the defeat of the Stamp Act, but their celebration was short. The following year, Parliament passed yet another series of laws "for asserting the Superiority of the Crown." Called the Townshend Acts, the laws imposed new duties, or taxes, on tea, lead, glass, and pigments for paint. Parliament also established a Royal Board of Commissioners responsible for enforcing the laws. The new law gave commissioners authority to search ships, homes, and businesses for illegally imported goods. Once

**The Townshend Acts gave customs officials the right to search people's homes for illegally imported goods.**

more, Boston reacted with anger. In the summer of 1768, a crowd attacked officials after they seized a ship owned by Patriot leader John Hancock.

British leaders had seen enough. They decided that British troops were needed to restore order in Boston. So it was that the Fourteenth and Twenty-ninth Regiments came to march through Boston on October 1, 1768.

One of the wealthiest merchants in New England, John Hancock was also an American Revolutionary leader. He would later become the first to sign the Declaration of Independence.

## SIGNS OF TROUBLE

Bostonians had seen British troops in their city before. Many soldiers had passed through the city during the French and Indian War to help defend the colonies. But this was different. This time, the soldiers had been sent to enforce unpopular laws and to maintain order. The people of Boston were proud of their ability to govern their own affairs and they resented the presence of troops in their city. As a local minister named Andrew Eliot put it: "To have a standing army! What can be worse to a people who have tasted the sweets of liberty?" Now the people of Boston would be living with soldiers all around them.

The first signs of trouble came when the soldiers began looking for lodgings. A British law called the Quartering Act required the colonies to provide barracks—places for soldiers to sleep. It also required the colonies to provide supplies for troops stationed there. The British commander in Boston, Colonel William Dalrymple, expected nothing less. However, he quickly learned that matters would not be so simple. His first step upon arriving was to meet with Royal Governor Francis Bernard. Bernard had been appointed governor by King

**Although the Quartering Act was not a direct tax on colonists, it served the same purpose. Colonists were forced to provide quarters, food, and transportation to British soldiers.**

George III, and Dalrymple expected Bernard's help in finding a place for his troops to stay.

Bernard was not able to offer Dalrymple much help. As governor, he had to work with the representatives of the people of Massachusetts. Bernard explained to Dalrymple that he could provide quarters for the troops only if Massachusetts lawmakers agreed. Those lawmakers made their feelings clear when they passed a resolution "to make no

Provision for the Troops in Boston, on any Pretense." The soldiers would have to find their own quarters.

The Twenty-ninth Regiment had tents with them, so they simply set up camp in Boston Common. The Fourteenth

**Appointed Royal Governor of Massachusetts in 1760, Sir Francis Bernard lost favor with the colonists after enforcing the Stamp Act and other British laws.**

**GOVERNING MASSACHUSETTS**

**The lawmaking body of Massachusetts was composed of two houses, or parts. The lower house, called the assembly, was elected by voters in town meetings. The assembly then elected the members of the second house, called the council. The governor had the right to approve or veto the assembly's choices for the council.**

Regiment wanted indoor quarters, so they forced open the doors of Faneuil Hall, the town meeting place. In the process, they also took hold of some 400 muskets that Patriot leaders had stored there. It wasn't until late October that Dalrymple finally moved the troops into an unused warehouse.

With the arrival of more troops, there were soon thousands of soldiers living in Boston. In their bright red coats, they stood out from the rest of the population. It became nearly impossible to walk the streets without encountering the soldiers, and the people of Boston were soon grumbling about the so-called redcoats. Relations between soldiers and citizens were tense. Soldiers were posted as **sentries** at

**FANEUIL HALL**

**Faneuil Hall opened in 1742 as a market where farmers and others could sell their produce. It also included public meeting rooms, and it quickly became a center of life in Boston. It still serves as a public market and meeting place today.**

**Faneuil Hall was the site of protests, speeches, and town meetings during the mid-1700s.**

British soldiers were a familiar sight on the streets of Boston.

public buildings around town. Bostonians who walked at night became used to soldiers, with bayonets ready, asking them, "Who goes there?"

To add to their meager army pay, some soldiers looked for part-time work in Boston. Boston's working men didn't like having to compete with the British for prized jobs. Soon, local boys mocked the red-coated soldiers by shouting "Lobsters!" at them. As tensions between citizens and soldiers increased, Governor Bernard found himself caught in the middle. Unable to satisfy either the army or local Patriots, he resigned his position in 1769. He was replaced by

Thomas Hutchinson. Hutchinson was born in the colonies and came from a wealthy Boston family. His term as governor would be every bit as rocky as Bernard's.

**Thomas Hutchinson was the last Royal Governor of the Massachusetts Bay Colony. He returned to England in 1774.**

## THE COMING CRISIS

By early 1770, Boston's boycott of British goods was losing some steam. More merchants defied the boycott and began stocking goods from England, seeking to make money from the sales. To stop them, Patriot leaders posted signs outside the merchants' shops identifying them as importers. Stores selling British goods became targets of vandalism and harassment.

On February 22, a sign reading "Importer" appeared outside the shop run by Theophilus Lillie. A neighbor named Ebenezer Richardson, who was known for being friendly to British officials, tried to take the sign down. Local boys began pelting Richardson with rocks. A crowd chased him to his home, where he tried to take cover. Stones began flying through Richardson's window, and one struck his wife.

To defend himself, Richardson fetched his musket. Appearing at an upstairs window, he warned the crowd to leave him alone. Then he fired into the crowd. An 11-year-old boy named Christopher Seider (sometimes called Snider) was hit, and soon died of his wounds. Richardson was arrested. Months later, he

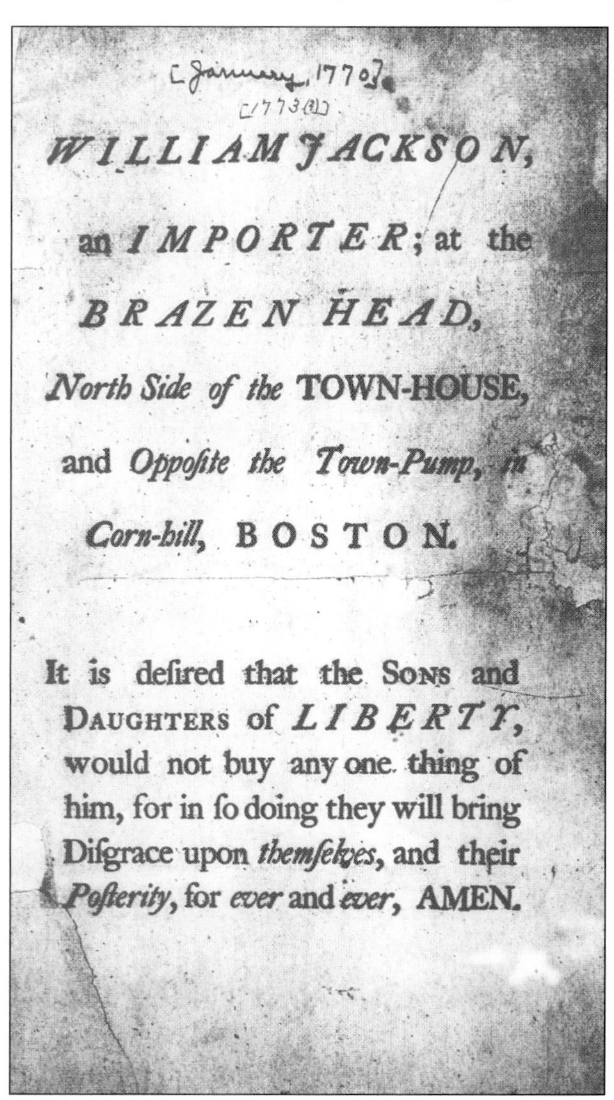
[January, 1770]

WILLIAM JACKSON,

an IMPORTER; at the

BRAZEN HEAD,

North Side of the TOWN-HOUSE,

and Oppoſite the Town-Pump, in

Corn-hill, BOSTON.

It is deſired that the SONS and DAUGHTERS of LIBERTY, would not buy any one thing of him, for in ſo doing they will bring Diſgrace upon themſelves, and their Poſterity, for ever and ever, AMEN.

**Patriots used documents such as this one to prevent people from buying goods from "traitors," or merchants who ignored the boycott on British goods.**

**A protest outside Lillie's Grocery led to the fatal shooting of an 11-year-old boy named Christopher Seider.**

stood trial and was convicted of murder. He served two years in prison before being **pardoned** by King George III.

Patriot leader Samuel Adams organized a grand funeral for Seider, hoping to use the boy's death to win support for the Patriot cause. At Seider's funeral, a crowd of 2,000 clamored for revenge. "Young as he was, he died in his country's cause," the *Boston Gazette* said of the boy.

Boston was a city on the brink of violence. Minister Andrew Eliot noted, "Things cannot remain in the state they are now in; they are hastening to a crisis. What will be the event, God knows."

## FIGHTING IN THE STREETS

Instead of calming Boston, the presence of British troops had only made the city more explosive. The soldiers became a symbol of British policies toward the colonies. Patriots unhappy with those policies aimed their anger at the soldiers. As they passed on the streets, citizens hurled insults at the redcoats. The soldiers responded with rude treatment and bullying.

It wasn't long before harsh words turned into blows. On March 2, 1770, a British soldier named Patrick Walker was strolling past a ropemaking plant near Milk Street. Ropemakers

**British soldiers arrest an American Patriot.**

often hired temporary workers, including sailors and soldiers who hoped to earn extra money. As Walker passed, a ropemaker asked him if was looking for work. When Walker said he was, the ropemaker insulted him by telling him he could clean his outhouse, or outdoor toilet. Walker shot back an insult of his own, and the two men took to fighting. Others joined in, and soon a brawl had broken out between soldiers and workmen.

**MAKING ROPE**

**The ropemaking factory—or ropewalk, as these factories were sometimes called—on Milk Street produced ropes and cables for use in the shipping business. The ropes were made from the strong fibers of the hemp plant. The fibers were dipped in hot tar, then stretched by hand around large spools to form ropes.**

The next day, the town was abuzz with talk of the fight. Some people thought the soldiers had been at fault, while others believed that the workmen had started it. All agreed that the fighting was not yet over.

By March 5, all of Boston was ready for something to happen. Snow lay a foot deep on the ground. Handbills, or posters, appeared on the streets, reading: "This is to Inform ye Rebellious People in Boston that ye Soldiers in ye Fourteenth and Twenty-ninth Regiments are determined to Joine together and defend themselves against all who shall oppose them." On King Street that night, Private Hugh White stood guard in front of Boston's Custom House.

Shortly after 8 P.M., a group of teenagers was gathered nearby. When a British officer passed, one of the boys insulted him, saying the officer owed his employer money. Private White came to the officer's defense, insisting that the officer was a gentleman. "There are no gentlemen in the British army," the boy replied. Angered, White raised his musket and struck the boy in the face with the butt end.

Attracted by the commotion, a crowd gathered and began to harass White. The private backed up to the steps of the Custom House as snowballs and chunks of ice began to fly at him. "Lousy rascal," the crowd jeered. "Kill him!" Fearing for his life, White called for help.

**A young apprentice shouted insults at a British officer, eventually prompting the officer to strike the boy with his rifle.**

## TRAGEDY ON KING STREET

Similar confrontations were taking place nearby. Blocks away, a crowd of citizens began pelting a group of soldiers with snowballs and rocks. More soldiers ran out from their barracks to join the fight, carrying shovels and bayonets. Their officers tried to restrain the men and hustled them back into the barracks. Meanwhile, the town's fire bells had begun to ring. With no fire department, Boston depended on volunteers to fight fires. When bells rang, citizens were expected to rush out onto the streets, carrying buckets and prepared to help fight a fire. But this night, the people of Boston seemed to know that the bells did not signal a fire. Many rushed out from homes and businesses carrying sticks and clubs, ready for a brawl.

**Captain Thomas Preston tried to restore order among the crowd, but that proved impossible.**

Private White remained under attack at the Custom House. About a block away, Captain Thomas Preston was in charge of the British main guard. Preston heard White's cry for relief, but probably feared that sending another squad of soldiers into the street would only make matters worse. It seemed as if a full-scale riot was about to break out. Still, the captain couldn't ignore White's plea for help. He assembled a squad of seven soldiers: Corporal William Wemms and Privates John Carroll, Matthew Kilroy, William Warren, Hugh Montgomery, James Hartigan, and William McCauley.

With Preston in the lead, they pushed and shoved their way through the crowd to the Custom House. There, they formed a line, with bayonets fixed and ready. At some point they loaded their muskets. As the crowd pressed in around them, Preston stood in front of his soldiers. He urged the crowd to disperse and go home. In response, he received curses and snowballs. Some witnesses said that as many as 300 to 400 people had gathered around the Custom House. Some dared the soldiers to fire.

A Boston man named Richard Palmes tried to act as peacemaker, and urged Preston not to shoot. Preston assured Palmes he would not give an order to fire, pointing out that he stood in front of his men's muskets. "If they fire, I will fall a sacrifice," he said.

But the crowd wanted a fight. Someone in the crowd threw a club toward the soldiers, and it struck Private Montgomery. Stunned and hurt, Montgomery fell to the ground

**Tensions escalated into an all-out riot, leaving five people dead. Patriots immediately dubbed the event "the Boston Massacre."**

and dropped his musket. Then he rose to his feet, picked up his weapon, and fired. Thinking an order to fire had been given, other soldiers began to fire their muskets. A sailor named Crispus Attucks was shot twice and killed. Laborer Sam Gray was killed by a gunshot to his head. Sailor James

**CRISPUS ATTUCKS**

**Crispus Attucks has become the best-known victim of the shootings on King Street. Some have called him "the first casualty of the American Revolution." Still, very little is known about Attucks. He is believed to have been of African and Native American ancestry. He may have been an escaped slave, and appears to have made his living as a sailor. In 1888, long after his death, a memorial to Attucks was erected in Boston Common.**

**Crispus Attucks, along with the other victims, became a symbol of liberty after the Boston Massacre.**

Today, a circle of cobblestones at Congress and State Streets marks the site of the Boston Massacre. The Old State House is in the background.

Caldwell was hit twice and fell. An apprentice named Samuel Maverick tried to run from the scene, but was shot and killed. Patrick Carr was struck in the hip and badly wounded. Six others lay in the street, wounded.

The crowd was stunned, as if it could not believe what had just happened. A witness named Joseph Hillyer said he didn't believe there were bodies on the ground. "I thought they'd been scared and run away, and left their greatcoats behind them." Some in the crowd ran; some tried to help the wounded. Meanwhile, Preston demanded to know why his men had fired. They told him they thought they had been ordered to fire. Preston quickly marched the squad back to the guard house.

As news spread of the tragedy, more people poured onto the streets. Governor Hutchinson rushed to the scene and appealed to the crowd to disperse. He promised the crowd that he would investigate the violence. He sent for justices Richard Dana and John Tudor, who quickly began interviewing witnesses. They issued a warrant for the arrest of Captain Preston. By 3 A.M., Preston was in jail. Hours later, the other eight soldiers present at the Custom House joined him. For the time being, Boston's streets were quiet.

**Samuel Adams was an outspoken critic of British policies. He organized several protests against British tax laws.**

## AFTER THE VIOLENCE

On Tuesday morning, March 6, another crowd had assembled. Led by Samuel Adams, thousands gathered outside Faneuil Hall to demand that British troops leave Boston. Hutchinson called a meeting of the council and agreed to meet with Boston civilian leaders. Adams and others told him the troops had to be removed from town. "Nothing can rationally be expected to restore the peace of the town and prevent blood and carnage but the immediate removal of the troops," read their demand. Hutchinson refused, however, insisting that he had no authority over the military. Colonel Dalrymple offered to remove one regiment from town, but Adams and the Patriots insisted that both regiments go. Finally,

**This painting by Howard Pyle shows Samuel Adams warning the British royal governor to remove British troops from Boston after the massacre.**

British soldiers left Boston after the shootings on March 5th.

Dalrymple and Hutchinson agreed that both regiments would be removed to Castle William in Boston Harbor.

On March 10, the Twenty-ninth Regiment marched to the Long Wharf, where ships waited to take them to Castle William. The Fourteenth Regiment followed the next day. It had been some eighteen months since they'd arrived in Boston, flags waving and drums beating. Now they were leaving to the sound of a jeering crowd along the Boston streets.

A Bostonian named Henry Pelham produced a drawing of the tragic events in front of the Custom House. Although the sketch got many details of the event wrong, it quickly became the most famous image of the tragedy. Silversmith Paul Revere made an **engraving** of the drawing, had it printed, and sold thousands of copies. It helped spread the fame of "the Boston Massacre."

**Paul Revere produced an engraving of the shootings. Despite containing several inaccuracies, it helped fuel anti-British sentiment.**

* * * *

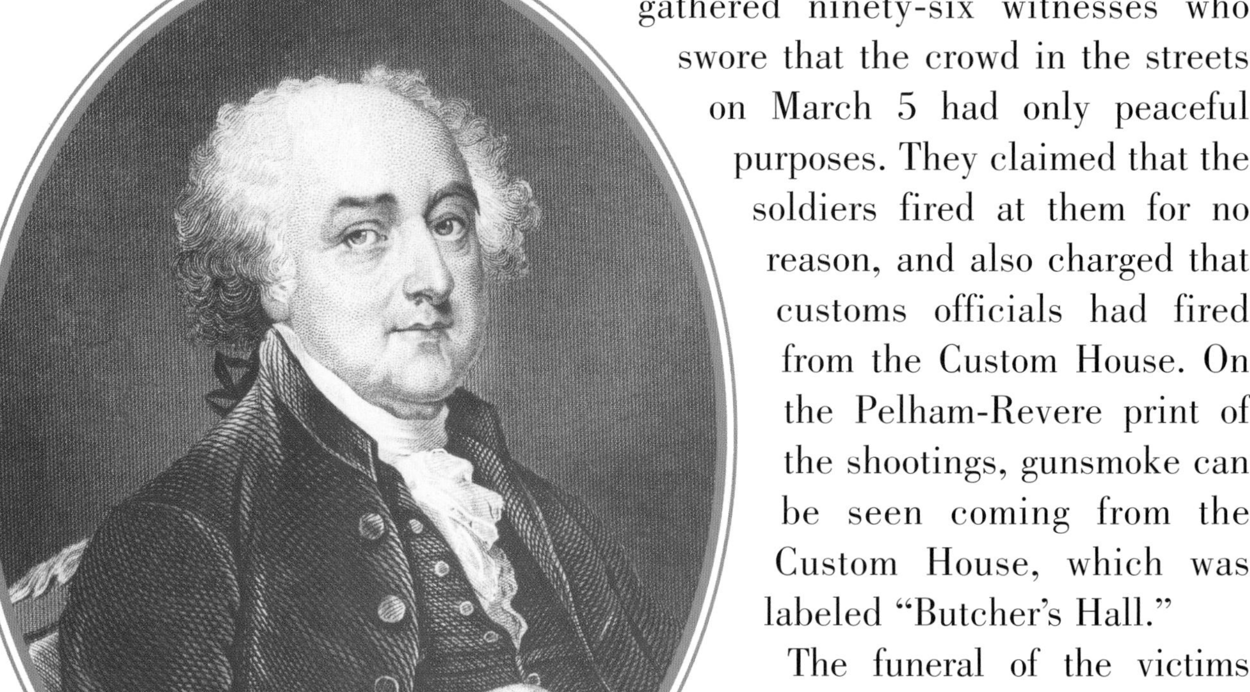
John Adams agreed to defend the soldiers to show that the colonists respected British law.

In the days after the shootings, Adams gathered ninety-six witnesses who swore that the crowd in the streets on March 5 had only peaceful purposes. They claimed that the soldiers fired at them for no reason, and also charged that customs officials had fired from the Custom House. On the Pelham-Revere print of the shootings, gunsmoke can be seen coming from the Custom House, which was labeled "Butcher's Hall."

The funeral of the victims stirred up public anger as well. Attucks, Maverick, Caldwell, and Gray were hailed as **martyrs** of the Patriot cause. (Carr died on March 14.) Their coffins were paraded through town, with thousands of people marching behind them. "O Americans! This Blood calls for **VENGEANCE!**" shouted the *Boston Gazette*.

As Samuel Adams was leading the Patriot response, his cousin John Adams was also being drawn into the case. The morning after the shootings, John Adams was visited by a Loyalist merchant named James Forrest. Forrest asked Adams to defend Captain Preston in court. Forrest told Adams that no other lawyer in Boston would take the case, fearing the anger of the Sons of Liberty. Adams' sympathies lay with the Patriots, and he knew that defending Preston would make him the target of public anger. Still, he couldn't refuse. Years later, he recalled: "I had no hesitation in answering . . . that Person whose Lives were at Stake ought to have the Council they preferred." Adams was later joined by Patriot Josiah Quincy, Jr., as lawyer for Preston and the eight soldiers.

Samuel Quincy was given the task of convicting the British soldiers of murder.

On March 12, prosecutor John Sewall began proceedings against the soldiers. Sewall presented an indictment, or statement of charges, to a grand jury. The indictment listed charges against Preston and the eight soldiers. It also listed charges against four **civilians** accused of firing into the crowd from the Custom House. It was the job of the grand jury to decide if the charges had enough merit to require a full trial. If not, the charges would be dismissed. The grand jury voted to try all of the accused for murder.

Prosecutor Sewall then left town mysteriously, so the court appointed Samuel Quincy to lead the prosecution of the soldiers. He was the brother of Josiah Quincy, Jr., who was working for the defense. Samuel Quincy was assisted by

Hours to the Gates of this City many Thouſands of our brave Brethren in the Country, deeply affected with our Diſtreſſes, and to whom we are greatly obliged on this Occaſion—No one knows where this would have ended, and what important Conſequences even to the whole Britiſh Empire might have followed, which our Modera-tion & Loyalty upon ſo trying an Occaſion, and our Faith in the Commander's Aſſurances have happily prevented.

Laſt Thurſday, agreeable to a general Requeſt of the Inhabitants, and by the Conſent of Parents and Friends, were carried to their *Grave* in Succeſſion, the Bodies of *Samuel Gray*, *Samuel Maverick*, *James Caldwell*, and *Criſpus Attucks*, the unhappy Victims who fell in the bloody Maſſacre of the Monday Evening preceeding!

SG SM JC CA

On this Occaſion moſt of the Shops in Town were ſhut, all the Bells were ordered to toll a ſolemn Peal, as were alſo thoſe in the neighboring Towns of Charleſtown Roxbury, &c. The Proceſſion began to move between the Hours of 4 and 5 in the Afternoon; two of the unfortunate Sufferers, viz. Meſſ. *James Caldwell* and *Criſpus Attucks*, who were Strangers, borne from Faneuil-Hall

**This obituary, or notice of death, appeared in the *Boston Gazette* on March 12, 1770. It named the four victims who died in the shootings on March 5th.**

Robert Treat Paine. For reasons that are still unclear, the court set up two separate trials—one for Preston, and one for the eight soldiers. By October 1770, the court was finally ready to begin the trial of Captain Thomas Preston.

## THE CAPTAIN'S TRIAL

On October 24, 1770, Captain Thomas Preston appeared in court to stand trial on the charge of murder. He entered a plea of not guilty. Preston was not on trial for killing anyone himself. Rather, prosecutors tried to show that by ordering his troops to fire, Preston was responsible for the deaths of the five men. Prosecutor Samuel Quincy opened the trial. He offered a summary of the evidence, or facts, that he would present to the jury, then called eight witnesses to the stand on the first day of the trial.

At the end of the day, the court was faced with an unusual problem. At the time, it was virtually unheard of for a trial to last more than one day. Yet, by nightfall, the prosecution had only just begun to present its case. What was to be done with the jurors overnight? Common sense called for them to be sequestered, or kept separate from the general population so

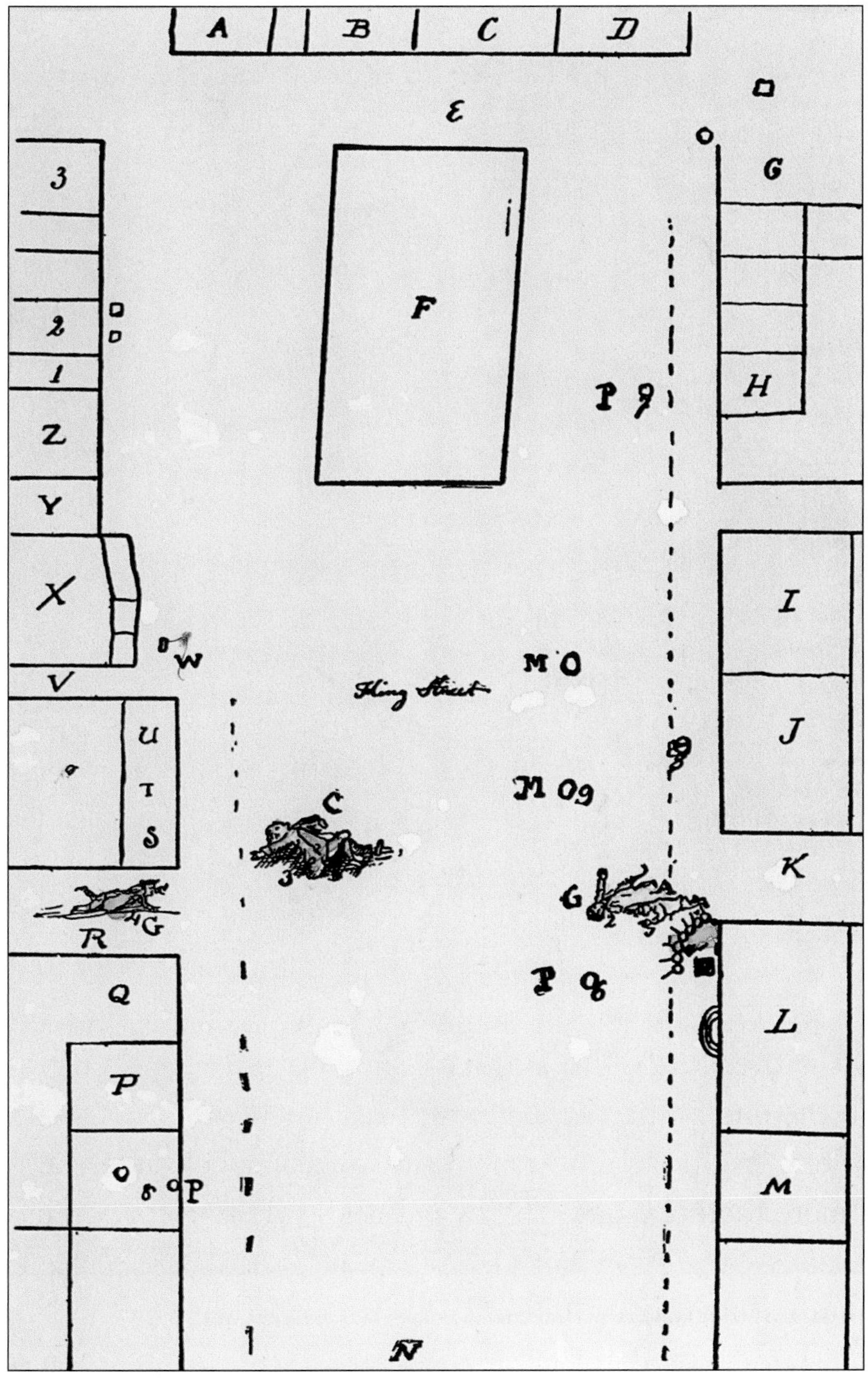


**Paul Revere's drawing of the Boston Massacre scene was used during the trial.**

**Lawyers for each side tried to portray the shootings in a different way.**

✶ ✶ ✶ ✶

they would not be influenced by events or arguments outside the courtroom. The prosecution and the defense were each allowed to name one keeper who would stay with the jury at the nearby house of the jail master.

As the trial continued, prosecutor Samuel Quincy called several witnesses who said they had heard Preston give the order to fire. However, some of these witnesses made errors in recalling the shootings. For example, one witness could not accurately describe what Preston was wearing that night. Mistakes such as these made it difficult to believe everything they said on the stand.

When the prosecutor finished calling witnesses, the defense was allowed to make its case. However, Preston was not allowed to testify in his own defense. Instead, the defense team called witnesses who said that they had heard someone else besides Preston give the order to fire. Joseph Hilyer testified that "the soldiers seemed to act pure nature . . . I mean they acted and fired by themselves." Others emphasized the confusion of the scene and the physical danger that the soldiers were under.

On October 29, the judges were ready to turn the case over to the jury for judgment. The next day, jurors announced that they had found Preston not guilty of murder. Preston was released from jail, and quickly moved to Castle William for his own safety. Boston remained calm, however. The trial of the eight soldiers still lay ahead.

## THE SOLDIERS' TRIAL

The jury's **verdict** of not guilty in the Preston trial seemed like bad news to the eight soldiers under his command. If Preston had not ordered them to fire, then common sense would suggest that the soldiers must have fired on their own. To many observers, the soldiers were clearly guilty of murder. What's more, Boston still expected someone to pay for the deaths of five citizens.

The soldiers' trial began on November 27, almost four weeks after the end of Preston's trial. The same four judges presided over both trials. The teams of defense and prosecution lawyers were much the same as well. Prosecutor Samuel Quincy began the trial by making a strong case against the soldiers. He called the shootings "the most melancholy event that has yet taken place on the continent of America." One witness testified that he saw Private Kilroy aim and shoot at Sam Gray. Another swore that he had heard Kilroy vowing to shoot Bostonians. Still another said that he had seen Kilroy walking around Boston with a bloody bayonet. Witnesses also testified that they had seen Private Montgomery shoot into the crowd.

However, witnesses disagreed on important details. Some said the shooting had begun before Montgomery was knocked down; some said after. Another witness admitted that many in the crowd that night were yelling "Fire!" at the soldiers. Still, Samuel Quincy told the jury that there was so much evidence against the soldiers that "you must pronounce them guilty."

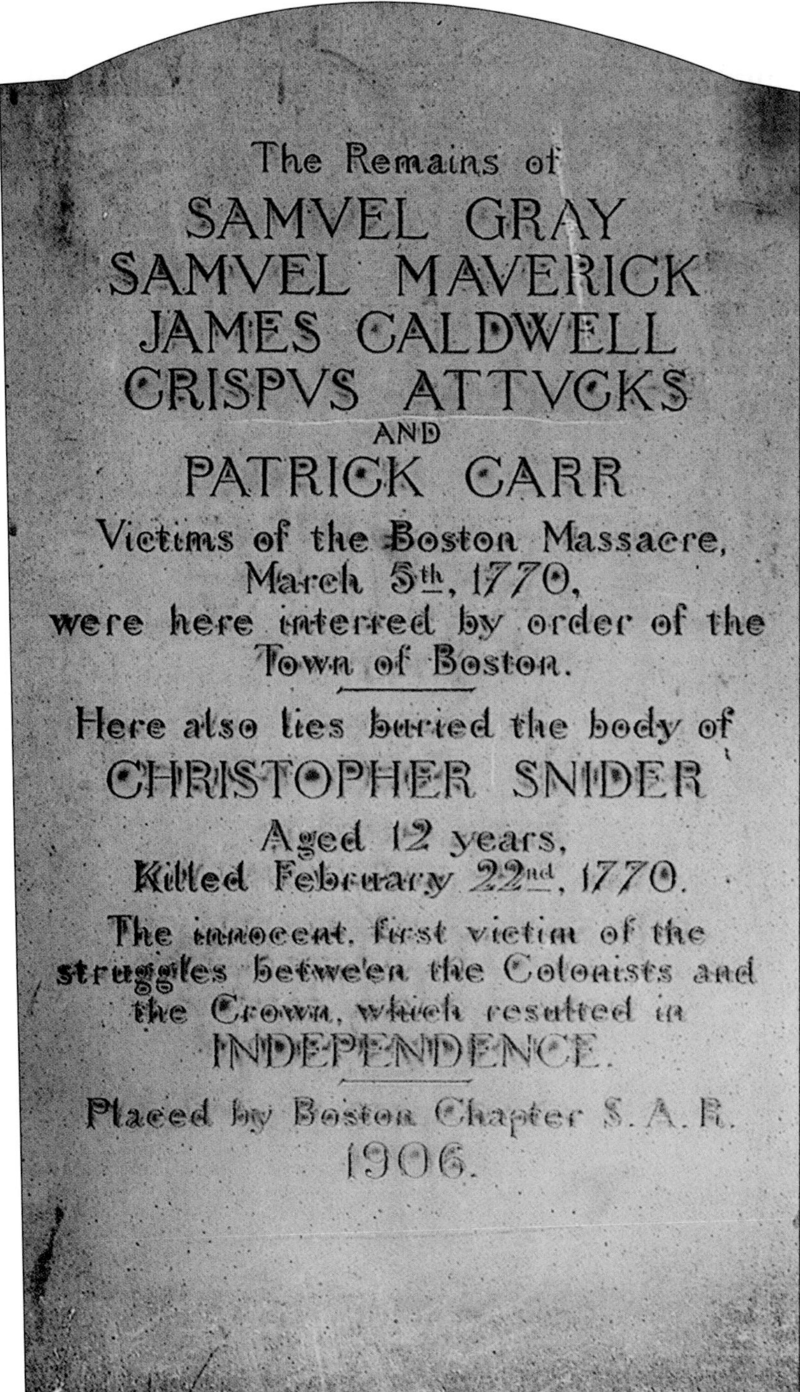


The remains of those who died during the Boston Massacre are buried in the Granary Burying Ground, now a stop along the Freedom Trail.

AMERICANS!
BEAR IN REMEMBRANCE
he HORRID MASSACRE
Perpetrated in King-ſtreet, BOSTON,
New-England,
n the Evening of March the Fifth, 177
When FIVE of your fellow countrymen,
RAY, MAVERICK, CALDWELL, ATTUCK
and CARR,
Lay wallowing in their Gore!
Being *baſely*, and moſt *inhumanly*
MURDERED!
And SIX others badly WOUNDED!
By a Party of the XXIXth Regiment,
nder the command of Capt. Tho. Preſto
REMEMBER!
That Two of the MURDERERS
Vere convicted of MANSLAUGHTER
By a Jury, of whom I ſhall ſay
NOTHING,
Branded in the hand!
And *diſmiſſed*,
The others were ACQUITTED,
And their Captain PENSIONED!
Alſo,
BEAR IN REMEMBRANCE
hat on the 22d Day of February, 177
The infamous
BENEZER RICHARDSON, Informer,
And tool to Miniſterial hirelings,
Moſt *barbarouſly*
MURDERED
HRISTOPHER SEIDER,
An innocent youth!
Of which crime he was found guilty
By his Country
On Friday April 20th, 1770;
But remained *Unſentenced*
n Saturday the 22d Day of February, 1772
When the GRAND INQUEST
For Suffolk county,
Were informed, at requeſt,
By the Judges of the Superior Court,
That EBENEZER RICHARDSON's *Caſe*
*Then lay before his* MAJESTY.
Therefore ſaid *Richardſon*
This day, MARCH FIFTH! 1772,
Remains UNHANGED!!!
Let THESE things be told to Poſterity!
And handed down
From Generation to Generation,
'Till Time ſhall be no more!
Forever may AMERICA be preſerved,
From weak and wicked monarchs,
Tyrannical Miniſters,
Abandoned Governors,
Their Underlings and Hirelings!
And may the
achinations of artful, *deſigning* wretches,
Who would ENSLAVE THIS People,
Come to an end,
Let their NAMES and MEMORIES
Be buried in eternal oblivion,
And the PRESS,
For a *SCOURGE* to Tyrannical Rulers,
Remain FREE.

**This notice was printed on March 5, 1772, in remembrance of the tragedy.**

★ ★ ★ ★

The defense lawyers tried to show that the soldiers acted in self-defense. They called on witnesses who said that the crowd on King Street had been threatening the soldiers. They reminded the jury of how people in the street were yelling "Kill them!" and how Private Montgomery had been knocked down. Surely, the soldiers couldn't be expected to stand there and take such abuse, Adams said. "Facts are stubborn things," he said in his closing statement. "If an assault was made to endanger their lives, the law is clear: They [the soldiers] had a right to kill in their own defense."

It took the jury two and a half hours to reach their verdict. They found six of the eight soldiers not guilty of murder. They found Privates Kilroy and Montgomery not guilty of murder, but guilty of manslaughter, a lesser charge. The six soldiers found not guilty were released that same day. Montgomery and Kilroy, however, could be sentenced to death for their crimes. To escape their punishment, they entered a plea for "benefit of clergy." In British law of the time, such a plea would allow first-time offenders to avoid their sentence. After being branded on their thumbs, the two soldiers were released. Later, the four customs officials accused of firing from the Custom House on March 5 were also found not guilty.

Although Boston accepted all these verdicts calmly, the fate of the five killed in the tragedy on King Street was not soon forgotten. For the next thirteen years, Boston observed a special day of mourning every March 5. Bells rang and

Soldiers Kilroy and Montgomery were branded with an "M" for murder on their right thumbs.

city leaders gave speeches in memory of the victims. Only after the United States had established itself as an independent nation did the memorials end. By then, the events of March 5, 1770, were seen as an important part of the struggle for independence from Great Britain. As John Adams later put it, "On that night, the foundation of American independence was laid."

## BENEFIT OF CLERGY

**The "benefit of clergy" was a privilege offered to ministers since the twelfth century. By entering such a plea, ministers could avoid punishment by civil courts. By the early 1700s, the privilege was extended to anyone convicted of a crime. However, the privilege could be used only once. Thus, criminals were branded on their thumbs to show that they had used the "benefit of clergy" plea.**

# Glossary

**boycott**—a joint effort to refuse to do business with a person, group, or country, usually as a way to express disapproval

**cargo**—goods delivered on a ship or by another form of transportation

**civilians**—people who are not members of the military

**delegate**—a person sent to represent or act on behalf of a group of people, such as at a political convention

**engraving**—a print created from a carving made in a hard surface

**faction**—a group of people who share common beliefs and act together

**imported**—brought into one country from another country to be sold

**martyr**—a person who gives up his or her life in support of a cause or belief

**mob**—a large, rowdy crowd

**pardoned**—freed from a penalty and allowed to avoid punishment

**repealed**—done away with by the action of a lawmaking body

**sentries**—soldiers standing guard at key places

**squadron**—a group of ships in military service

**treasury**—the government department in charge of finances, or the government's supply of wealth

**unconstitutional**—not following the principles set down in the constitution of a state or nation

**vengeance**—punishment made in exchange for an insult or injury

**verdict**—a judgment or decision reached by a jury

# Timeline: The Boston

| 1754 | 1763 | 1764 | 1765 | 1767 | 1768 |
|---|---|---|---|---|---|
| The French and Indian War begins. | The French and Indian War ends, with Great Britain winning control of North America. | British Parliament passes the Sugar Act. | British Parliament passes the Stamp Act; widespread protests in American colonies follow. | British Parliament passes the Townshend Acts. | The Fourteenth and Twenty-ninth Regiments of the British army arrive in Boston to impose law and order. |

# Massacre

## 1770

**MARCH 5**
British soldiers fire on a crowd in Boston, killing five.

**OCTOBER 24**
The trial of Captain Preston begins.

**OCTOBER 30**
Captain Preston is found not guilty of murder.

**NOVEMBER 27**
The trial of the other eight soldiers begins.

**DECEMBER 5**
The soldiers are found not guilty of murder; Privates Kilroy and Montgomery are found guilty of manslaughter.

**DECEMBER 14**
At sentencing, Kilroy and Montgomery plead "benefit of clergy" and are released.

## 1771

The first memorial observance of the Boston Massacre takes place.

# To Find Out More

## BOOKS

Harness, Cheryl. *The Revolutionary John Adams*. Washington, DC: National Geographic, 2003.

Jones, Veda Boyd. *Samuel Adams: American Patriot*. Philadelphia: Chelsea House, 2001.

Lukes, Bonnie. *The Boston Massacre*. San Diego: Lucent Books, 1998.

Sakurai, Gail. *The Thirteen Colonies*. New York: Children's Press, 2000.

## ONLINE SITES

The Boston Massacre Files
*http://www.bostonmassacre.net*

Liberty! The American Revolution
*http://www.pbs.org/ktca/liberty*

# Index

**Bold** numbers indicate illustrations.

# About the Author

**Andrew Santella's** work has appeared in the *New York Times Book Review, GQ,* and many other publications. He is also the author of a number of nonfiction books for young readers. Mr. Santella lives outside Chicago.